IMAGES
of America

GARRARD COUNTY
in WORLD WAR II

This book is dedicated to the young men who left their beautiful Garrard County homeland
from 1940 to 1945 to serve their country during World War II.
Then-Pvt. Daniel Glenmore Dailey, at 19, was one of those brave young men.
While stationed at Fort Sill, Oklahoma, he wrote this poem:

KENTUCKY

Soon I'll be going
Where the soft wind is blowing
In Kentucky.
Things will be blooming
When I roam where there is room
In Kentucky.

Where the sky is blue
And the grass is too.
And the sunniest style
Of welcoming smile
Is made to order for you.
Somebody's waiting
To begin celebrating
In Kentucky.

I'm not denying
That my heart will be flying
When I get to Kentucky.
I'll declare it's heaven
To dream of all those wonders in store.
Oh, Lord, make me lucky
When I get to Kentucky,
Let me stay there forever more.

Pfc. Daniel Glenmore Dailey, photographed here during basic training at Fort Sill, was killed in action in Germany before reaching his 21st birthday. The above poem was found in his billfold and sent to his mother, Beatrice Casey Dailey, of Buckeye. In large part because of the sentiments expressed in this poem, his family asked to have his body returned to Garrard County, where he was buried with full military honors in Lancaster Cemetery—in Kentucky. (Courtesy George Dailey.)

IMAGES
of America

GARRARD COUNTY
in WORLD WAR II

Rita Mackin Fox

Published by Arcadia Publishing
Charleston SC, Chicago IL, Portsmouth NH, San Francisco CA

Printed in Great Britain

Library of Congress Catalog Card Number: 2005930283

For all general information contact Arcadia Publishing at:
Telephone 843-853-2070
Fax 843-853-0044
E-mail sales@arcadiapublishing.com
For customer service and orders:
Toll-Free 1-888-313-2665

Visit us on the Internet at www.arcadiapublishing.com

ABOUT THE AUTHOR

Rita Mackin Fox was born in 1958 in Louisville, Kentucky. She lived for 14 years in the Finger Lakes region of New York State before returning to Kentucky 10 years ago and buying a home in Garrard County. Soon after earning her bachelor of arts degree in journalism at Eastern Kentucky University, she began working as an editorial assistant at Berea College and founded the quarterly magazine *Paint Lick Reflections* in April 2002. *Garrard County in World War II* is her second book for Arcadia Publishing, the first of which, Images of America: *Garrard County*, was published in August 2005. She is working with Margaret Creech Burkett on a comprehensive World War II history of the county, as well as exploring the possibilities of proposing more Arcadia books on Nelson County and Louisville, the birthplaces of her parents, Joseph and Mary Jane Head Mackin.

CONTENTS

ACKNOWLEDGMENTS

Once again, I was aided substantially in this project by my sidekick, Margaret Creech Burkett, whose research helped me and the family members of veterans fill the gaps of knowledge about their service with her many hours spent poring over the pages of the *Central Record*'s 1940–1946 editions in the summer of 2005. In fact, she found so much material, I am encouraging her to compile a comprehensive history of the county's World War II servicemen, for which I will be her sidekick for a change.

I am also grateful to the members of the Disabled American Veterans (DAV) Chapter 25 at Lancaster for their hospitality and willingness to share photographs and stories with me.

The crewmembers of the USS *Garrard* and their families provided the photographs for that chapter. Special thanks go to Robert Wiedel, who mailed me his original photographs.

Aileen Reed at the Garrard County Historical Society's Jail Museum shared an excellent collection of photographs and memorabilia from the USS *Garrard*, including shipmate Kenneth Billings's memorabilia.

Janice Burdette Blythe invited Margaret and me to the 2005 Mason High School Reunion and shared her father James Burdette's four World War II–era scrapbooks of the Occupation of Japan era.

The members of the Daughters of the American Revolution's James Garrard Chapter are to be commended for their efforts to identify and honor those from this county who served in World War II.

I am indebted to the staff of the Garrard County Public Library for letting me set up shop so many days to scan photographs and for their many scrapbooks and World War II reference books.

The Friends of Paint Lick also allowed me to set up and scan photographs in their center.

My pen pal, Sonja Schmitz-Wagner, in Bonn, Germany, offered to help identify locations in photographs taken in Germany and to photograph grave sites at U.S. military cemeteries there. Young Germans are anxious to learn more about the war.

The current and former staff of the *Central Record* newspaper are to be applauded for writing about the men and women of World War II during the war and ever since.

I am grateful to all who brought me images to scan, often on behalf of other veterans and family members. Special thanks go to Doan Adkison, Margaret Burkett, Wilma Cornelius, and Vera Renfro, who took the initiative to gather many photographs from throughout their neighborhoods, towns, or extended families. Their commitment to honoring as many veterans as possible was inspiring.

And most especially, thank you to the World War II veterans from Garrard County for their service to this nation and for being such great ambassadors for their home county while doing so. As my readers will learn from their stories, freedom is not free.

INTRODUCTION

World War II was the largest and most violent armed conflict in history. This book is intended to continue the chronicling of Garrard County's war years, but only tells about a small number of the more than 725 men and women who served from this county. Much already has been lost, but the author hopes that the photographs here will inspire more veterans to share their stories and photographs with younger generations. She encourages family members to record these stories, on tape or in writing, to be treasured by family members and Garrard Countians for many years to come and would love for readers to share those stories with her for future publications.

The book begins the story in chapter one with basic-training camp, where all who served in the military began their active service. Those who continued to train and served stateside are included here as well.

Chapter two looks at the Asiatic-Pacific Theater, which included the entire Pacific Rim. For many, it was a time to get primitive. Sgt. James Baker, born in Nina and serving with the army's 41st Division in the South Pacific, recalled an experience during the intensive fighting on Biak Island in Dutch New Guinea. He went three days without food and slept standing up. Then he and some of his buddies came upon a big hole in the ground in which a 300-pound wild boar was trapped. He said, "Boys, there's our supper." They laughed and asked how he expected to get him out of the hole. Country boy Baker showed them by tying a rope around the wild pig and helping as several guys pulled it out. They ate well that day.

In chapter three, we look at the war in Europe and North Africa. While the draft was reinstated in 1940, at least one county man didn't wait for the U.S. to enter the war. Forestus Reid Lear joined the Royal Canadian Air Force early in 1941. After Pearl Harbor was attacked, America joined the fight against Japan and Germany. In an August 1944 letter published in the *Central Record*, Roy Browning, of Paint Lick, wrote from France: "A few nights before, the Americans captured a large number of German tanks, trucks, motorcycles, guns, and bicycles on the road and they found new suits of clothes, . . . blankets with the tags still on them, and many other things showing that the Germans are still well supplied." Fighting continued for about eight more months before the Germans surrendered. He was right.

News like this from the battlefields spurred Garrard County residents back home to make many sacrifices to help support the men and women in uniform for the long haul. Chapter four focuses on how residents kept the home fires burning with war-bond rallies; parties for troops passing through; collections of tin, rubber, cardboard, and other items for the war effort; bandage rolling at the Red Cross; and writing letters to the troops to boost their morale.

As a result of county residents exceeding their war bond sales by more than $100,000 in 1943, the government named a navy transport ship the USS *Garrard* after their home. Chapter five is dedicated to the men who served on this ship and includes photographs and stories contributed by several of the shipmates. Survivors of the crew, as well as one of the former POWs liberated from Japan, held a reunion in Garrard County in 2002. Crewmembers established a scholarship program to support high-school youth in the county.

Chapter six deals with the end of the war and the occupation periods in Germany and Japan immediately after the war. Army soldier Edwin Sutton of Drake's Creek, who was stationed in Greenland during the war, expressed his emotions about the rumors of the war's end in an August 14, 1945, letter home: "The way I feel is like getting on my knees and giving thanks that Oscar [his brother] & myself got through safe and will be coming home again to stay for good soon." Garrard County sent more than 725 men and women to serve during this war. Still other county natives enlisted or were drafted from outside Garrard. No family was untouched by the heartache of sending a loved one off to fight or of learning that a family member or neighbor had died. All shared in the joy of welcoming home those who survived.

But "the real heroes didn't come home," said Thomas B. Scott, a World War II veteran and member of the county's Disabled American Veterans Chapter 25 in Lancaster. Some made the ultimate sacrifice and gave all in service to their country. The forever-young faces of 15 of those who were killed in action are shown in chapter seven. While the official casualty list for Garrard is 23 names, the war memorial at the courthouse honors 39, including some who moved away from the county prior to the war. The James Garrard Chapter of the Daughters of the American Revolution keeps their memory alive at memorial services. But while working on this book, more names were found and added to the list, which stands at 48 at the time of publication. The last page of this book lists them, including those who died in battle and from wounds, as well as those in service during the war and occupation period who died of illness or accidents. The list probably will continue to grow as research continues.

In Sutton's August 1945 letter, he said it best: "There were many a man that lost his life fighting for this day, and I don't see how they can ever be forgotten." Neither do I.

—Rita Mackin Fox

KEY TO CONTRIBUTORS

Barry Adams, Lancaster, KY
Doan and Mary "Pug" Adkison, Lancaster, KY
Maryann Ramsey Alquist, Wapiti, WY
Janice Turner Amon, Lancaster, KY
Cecil Arnold, Lancaster, KY
Walter Lee "Pete" Arnold, Lancaster, KY
James and Doris Barker Baker, Lancaster, KY
Nora Rhodus Bethel, Lexington, KY
Janice Burdette Blythe, Berea, KY
Mary Ann McQuerry Bolton, Lancaster, KY
Woodford Bowling, Lancaster, KY
John Boyle, Lancaster, KY
Kevin Brickey, Lancaster, KY
J. C. and Reva Broaddus, Lancaster, KY
Connie Jennings Brown, Paint Lick, KY
Michael Browning, Lancaster, KY
Margaret Creech Burkett, Paint Lick, KY
Ollie Ball "Ricki" Collett, Crab Orchard, KY
Don Combs, Berea, KY
William Combs, Berea, KY
Wilma Montgomery Cornelius, Lancaster, KY
Nancy Conn Cox, Hillsboro, OH
Reba Cotton, Lancaster, KY
George Dailey, Lancaster, KY
Lloyd Dailey, Lancaster, KY
Bob Day, Berea, KY
Peggy Teater Derringer, Lancaster, KY
Disabled American Veterans Chapter 25,
 Lancaster, KY
Jim Drake, Berea, KY
Arthur and Mary Dunn, Lancaster, KY
Inez Dyehouse, Lancaster, KY
Delbert and Brenda Eason, Lancaster, KY
Rhonda Wilmot Ellis, Berea, KY
David Feldman, Lancaster, KY
Eugene and Rita Finley, Paint Lick, KY
Darwin Foley, Shelbyville, KY
Garrard County Jail Museum, Lancaster, KY

Charles Ernest Glenn, Lancaster, KY
Ron Goens, Lancaster, KY
Earl and Gary Goodwin, Greenfield, IN
Ella Mae Combs Green, Berea, KY
Lorene Green, Berea, KY
Ethel Turner Gross, Berea, KY
Sharon Cotton Hamilton, Lancaster, KY
Geneva Bryant Harrison, Berea, KY
Paula Christopher Hatfield, Lancaster, KY
Lorraine Hatfield, Harrodsburg, KY
Raymond "Dee" Hatfield, Lancaster, KY
Phyllis Wilmot Hicks, Lancaster, KY
Nellie Conn Hightower, Harrodsburg, KY
Roger Kirkpatrick, Mobile, AL
Jackie Combs Lake, Berea, KY
Edwin Land, Lancaster, KY
David and Frances Layton, Lancaster, KY
Jerome Layton, Berea, KY
Fred Lear, Lancaster, KY
Dan Ledford, Paint Lick, KY
Dorothy Baierlein Lynch, Danville, KY
Mitzi Conn Makenas, Vandalia, OH
Ruth Wilson McElveen, New Albany, IN
Robin and Wendell Metcalf, Lancaster, KY
Janie Ramsey Miller, Lancaster, KY
Mom Blakeman's Candy Inc., Lancaster, KY
Tommy Montgomery, Lancaster, KY
Lynn Guyn Murphy, Lexington, KY
Betty Rich Norment, Henderson, KY
Roy Patterson, Lancaster, KY
Barry Peel, Lancaster, KY
Gladys and Joe Pitts Jr., Berea, KY
Eugene Pollard, Danville, KY
Donna Murphy Powell, Lancaster, KY
J. T. Prewitt, New Castle, KY
Harold Scott Ralston, Tipp City, OH
Jim Rankin, Danville, KY
Harold and Vera Meadows Renfro, Berea, KY

Clellagene Rhodus and sons, Paint Lick, KY
Lucille Rich, Uniontown, KY
Norma Rich, Uniontown, KY
Katie Alexander Rollins, Paint Lick, KY
Jim Schooler, Lancaster, KY
Family of Bluford Sebastian, Stanford, KY
Peggy Cox Sharp, Lancaster, KY
Geneva Green Starnes, Paint Lick, KY
Paul and Helen Starnes, Paint Lick, KY
Ralph and Thelma Parson Starnes, Paint Lick, KY
Barbara Hurt Todd, Lancaster, KY

Mike and Phyllis Tracy, Lancaster, KY
Betty Meadows Tudor, Richmond, KY
Christine Tudor, Danville, KY
Shirley Montgomery Turner, Lancaster, KY
Norma Vanoy, Lancaster, KY
Susie Prewitt Vasquez, Harrodsburg, KY
Robert Wiedel, Titusville, FL
Judy Sutton Williams, Lancaster, KY
Paul Wilson family, Lancaster, KY
Betty Wood, Lancaster, KY
Wes Zanone, Lexington, KY

SOURCES

Arnold, Cecil. *Lancaster Cemetery Book*. Utica, KY: McDowell Publications, 1995.
Central Record 1940–1946, Lancaster, KY.
Vockery, Bill and Kathy Vockery. *1930 Garrard County Census*. Lancaster, KY: Garrard County Historical Society, 2004.
———. *Garrard County Cemetery Book*. Lancaster, KY: Garrard County Historical Society, 1997.

On the Cover: The 486th Bombardier Group, 3rd Air Division, flew 30 missions in B-17 and B-24 bombers. This division was cited by the president for its England to Africa shuttle bombing of the Messerschmitt factories at Regensburg, Germany. Posing in front of a B-24 from left to right are (first row) Rodrigo B. Rodriguez (gunner, Connecticut), Walter F. Alemidea (armored gunner, Massachusetts), Ralph Starnes (engineer gunner, Paint Lick, Kentucky), Jack B. Niedner (radio operator, Missouri), Richard E. Hurley (assistant radio gunner, Idaho), and Louis A. Rheaume (assistant armored gunner, Connecticut); (back row) Lt. George W. Oldham (bombardier, New Jersey), Lt. Nathaniel W. Holman (navigator, New Jersey), Lt. Paul A. Lyons (pilot, Vermont), Lt. Harold E. Jernigan (copilot, North Carolina). (Courtesy Ralph and Thelma Starnes.)

One

BASIC TRAINING AND STATESIDE SERVICE

Not knowing what lay ahead of them, the biggest worry some of the boys had when shipped off to training camps was whether their girlfriends would wait for them. This postcard was sent from Nathan Prewitt in Camp Shelby, near Hattiesburg, Mississippi, to his girlfriend, Allene Conn. The two were later married. (Courtesy Susie Vasquez.)

The story of basic training for World War II really began during the years leading up to the war in the Civilian Conservation Corps (CCC). Here Woods Walker Lear, left, and an unidentified CCC member in Idaho lived in barracks, did construction and conservation projects, and became disciplined to military life. Lear later served and was killed in World War II at Leyte Island in the Philippines. (Courtesy Fred Lear.)

Luther Gilbert Creech also trained at a CCC Camp. He later joined the navy and was on the USS *Chicago* when it sank off a coast in the Solomon Islands. Fellow Garrard Countian Jasper Donald Sebastian was on the USS *Montpelier*, which picked up Creech and other survivors. (Courtesy Margaret Burkett.)

Four of many thousands of inductees at Fort Thomas in Northern Kentucky are, from left to right, James Ross, Ralph Starnes, James Baker, and an unidentified soldier from West Virginia. Many of the boys from Garrard County began their service here. Starnes and Baker of Garrard County joined the army air forces and army infantry respectively. (Courtesy James Baker.)

Isidor J. Feldman took basic training at Fort Bragg, North Carolina. In the early years, once soldiers and sailors were inducted, they were sent home to straighten out their personal affairs and then reported to their local draft board (No. 49 in Garrard County). In later years, they went directly from induction to the reception center and then to basic training. (Courtesy David Feldman.)

Accommodations at military bases like Camp Beale, near Chico, California, were spartan, but much more comfortable than what was to come. Many camps offered entertainment and recreation as well. At left, Army Air Force trainee William Smith reads a newspaper as bunkmate Dan Ledford relaxes in the top bunk. Ledford, of Manse, was stationed here from 1942 until 1944, when he shipped out to New Guinea. His wife, Laverne, moved here to be near her husband and worked in nearby Chico. Below, troops at Camp Beale march in formation on the base. (Courtesy Dan Ledford.)

Harry O. Eason (right) and an unidentified buddy nicknamed "Armstrong" trained at the Army Air Force Flexible Gunnery School in Kingman, Arizona. Eason was probably an airplane mechanic. Before advancing to airplane guns, though, trainees started with BB guns, progressed to shotguns, and worked their way up to the more advanced weaponry of the Army Air Force. (Courtesy Delbert Eason.)

Standing outside Ellis Bell's home in Paint Lick, cousins Vernis "Bunny" Green (left) and Elmore Green of Cartersville enjoy a reunion. Vernis trained at Camp Bowier, Texas, and at the Medical Department Station Hospital, Camp Swift, in Bastrop, Texas. (Courtesy Lorene Green and Jim Drake.)

Cpl. Harold D. Murphy enlisted in the U.S. Marine Corps on July 14, 1943, and in the summer of 1944, he was serving as a propeller mechanic with the 9th Marine Aircraft Wing, which was in combat training at Cherry Point, North Carolina. He later served in the Asiatic Pacific Theater, where this photograph was taken. (Courtesy Donna Powell.)

Pfc. Robert "Bob" Meadows of the army trained at Fort Eustis, Virginia, then attended anti-aircraft artillery school at Fort Bliss, Texas, and also trained at Camp Haan, California. He served in the Hawaiian Islands and was in the service from 1943 through 1945. (Courtesy Betty Tudor.)

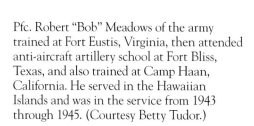

Pfc. Dan Ledford (left) and Mail Specialist Third Class Ralph Spillman, both of the Paint Lick area, enjoy a visit at Camp Beale Army Air Force Base in Chico, California. Spillman worked in the navy's postal service operation from December 1942 to 1946, moving from ship to ship and on land. While at a California receiving station, he looked up his friend, Ledford. (Courtesy Dan Ledford.)

An army travels on its stomach, and there to make sure the troops were well fed were men like T4g. Wilson J. "Shorty" Browning of Nina. Browning, who trained at the Bakers and Cooks School in Fort Jay, New York, served with the 346th Infantry in the Rhineland and Central Europe campaigns. Cooks pulled double duty, and he also trained as a rifleman. (Courtesy Michael Browning.)

John Boyle of Lowell (far right) and unidentified trainees pose at Camp Wheeler, Georgia, on a work detail in 1942 soon after arriving at basic training. (Courtesy John Boyle.)

Grover Schooler Jr., right, and an unidentified buddy are shown here, possibly while training in Missouri. Not only did they wear leather bomber jackets but also leather pants. Schooler's basic training was at Camp Benjamin Harrison in Indiana. In Boston, before heading to Germany, he met his future wife at a USO party. The two were married in June 1946, soon after he returned stateside. (Courtesy Jim Schooler.)

Bob Day went into the navy the same day his friend and Cartersville-area neighbor, Harold Renfro (below), did. They trained at Sampson, New York. Day was training on one side of the hill and Bob on the other. "We set down in the holler and hollared at each other," said Renfro. (Courtesy Bob Day.)

"We never knew where we were going after basic or why," Harold Renfro shared with the author in the summer of 2005. "I just got off the train in Bedford, Pennsylvania, and went to a big resort hotel for radio training." Renfro served in the Western Pacific theater as a radioman. (Courtesy Harold and Vera Renfro.)

Machinist's Mate Second Class Robert Russell Conn was working at the Philadelphia Naval Shipyard when the war broke out. He joined the navy and trained at Great Lakes Naval Training Center in Illinois. He returned to the shipyard and worked on the catapults that launched planes from aircraft carriers. Throughout his service (1942–1946), he was sent around the world to service catapults. After his discharge, he continued this work for the navy as a civilian. (Nellie Hightower.)

Sgt. Irvine Phelps Stapp Jr. was assigned to B-29 combat crew training, which began in December 1944 at Lowry Field in Denver, Colorado, and continued at Buckingham Army Air Field Flexible Gunnery School in Fort Myers, Florida. He graduated in the spring of 1945 and continued to train in Tucson, Arizona, and Topeka, Kansas, before being assigned to a B-29 crew headed overseas in August 1945. (Courtesy Ann Blevins via Kevin Brickey.)

On July 25, 1943, William Cliff Ledford (left) clowns around, holding a rifle on an unidentified friend, and writes: "In front of our barracks—I am making Logan tell it. Ha!" The war ended before Ledford was sent overseas. At one point, perhaps in this photograph, Ledford was stationed at the Flexible Gunnery School at Loredo (Texas) Army Air Field. (Courtesy Dan Ledford.)

Cpl. Sallie Lee Conn was one of 150,000 American women who served in the Women's Army Corps (WACs). Stationed at Fort Hood, Texas, she worked in the motor pool. The army began recruiting WACs in 1942. Two other women's corps were the navy's WAVEs (Women Accepted for Volunteer Emergency Service) and the U.S. Army Air Force's WAAFs (Women's Army Air Force). (Courtesy Nancy Cox.)

Neighbors and friends back on Copper Creek, Joe Pitts Jr., left, and Ernest Chasteen trained together at Camp Green Bay in Great Lakes, Illinois. Pitts sent this photo postcard to Harold Renfro in December 1943 and wrote, "Camp Green Bay, a fun place to be. Ha ha." Renfro later joined the navy as well. (Courtesy Harold Renfro; information Gladys and Joe Pitts Jr.)

Most soldiers and sailors were given a leave just before shipping out overseas. Here Sgt. Smith Ledford, G. B. Robinson, and Pfc. Dan Ledford share a leave at Manse before Robinson shipped out to England and Ledford to New Guinea. Dan's brother, Smith, remained stateside during the war. (Courtesy Betty Tudor.)

Woodford Bowling (seated), of Paint Lick, cuts up with some unidentified buddies at Camp Blanding in Stark, Florida, in 1944. The building at right is one of the five-man huts they lived in. The mess hall is the white building behind them. (Courtesy Woodford Bowling.)

Joe Smith, of Monticello, Kentucky, and Woodford Bowling and Loraine "Red" Sowder, both of Paint Lick, are shown here at Camp Blanding, Florida. When Bowling saw his friend's induction paper stamped "Army," he asked to be army, too, "so that I could stay with Red." Sowder was sent to Europe and later received minor wounds. Bowling trained as a bazooka man at Camp McCoy, Wisconsin. He left Boston on Thanksgiving Day 1944 and was wounded in the Rhineland campaign. (Courtesy Woodford Bowling.)

Sgt. Robert Guyn (far right) was stationed at one time in Dayton, Ohio, and is seen here with other airmen and WAAFs on a WAAF recruiting trip at a resort in French Lick, Indiana. Next to him is Florence LeBeaux, of Abbeyville, Louisiana. The others are not identified. (Courtesy Lynn Murphy.)

Raymond Douglas "Dee" Hatfield of Lancaster trained men at the officer candidate school at Fort Benning, Georgia, in 1945–1946. The accelerated officer-training program took about three months, resulting in its graduates being referred to as "90-day wonders." Here he is standing outside the store run by his father, Wesley Hatfield, in Lancaster. (Courtesy Raymond Hatfield.)

Wesley Thompson of Buena Vista joined the merchant marines with parental consent at 16. His chaplain at the U.S. Maritime Service Training Station in Sheepshead Bay, Brooklyn, New York, wrote his mother, Delphy Thompson, on June 12, 1945: "We are happy to tell you that he participated today in a religious graduation service. Men who desire it are given a New Testament, a USO kit of devotional materials, and Holy Communion." (Courtesy Wilma Cornelius.)

Pvt. Joe Clinton "J. C." Turner of Buckeye guarded German POWs in Florida and possibly Georgia. Here he is during basic training at Camp Blanding, Florida. (Courtesy Wilma Cornelius.)

The first platoon of Company E, 271st Infantry, has just completed training at Camp Shelby in August 1943. Camp Shelby, near Hattiesburg, Mississippi, was named by members of the first troops to train here during World War I, the 38th Division, in honor of Isaac Shelby, a Revolutionary War hero and first governor of Kentucky. (Courtesy Jackie Lake.)

The only person identified in the group photograph above is Paint Lick's Pfc. George W. Combs Jr., who is at the far left in the second row. In the close-up at left, he is in the first row, left. Combs was killed in action at St. Lô, France, one year to the month after this photograph was taken and only six weeks after he arrived in the European theater of operations. (Courtesy Jackie Lake.)

Two

ASIATIC PACIFIC THEATER

Servicemen didn't abandon their faith while in the military. If anything, their faith grew stronger. Chaplains were in every unit, and chapels, like this one in New Guinea, sprung up whenever troops were stationed for long periods of time in one place. (Courtesy Dan Ledford.)

When the Japanese attacked Pearl Harbor on December 7, 1941, Oscar Sutton was on the Pearl Harbor–based aircraft carrier USS *Enterprise*. Fortunately the carrier was returning from Wake Island and still 215 miles from base when the attack came in Hawaii. The ship was ordered to steam out to sea and wait until dark before returning. Sutton joined the navy in December 1940, a member of the Fighting 6, serving for six years. He fought in the Coral Sea, Midway, New Hebrides, and Guadalcanal. (Courtesy Judy Williams.)

Sgt. Walter D. Rich of Fall Lick was stationed with the army at Pearl Harbor on the "Day of Infamy." He remembers the surprise, pandemonium, disbelief, and gratefulness of having survived. For the families of both Rich and Oscar Sutton (above), it was many weeks of uncertainty after the attack before they knew their loved ones indeed had survived. From here, Rich was sent to France and Germany. (Courtesy Lucille Rich and Betty Norment.)

Yeoman First Class James Thomas Prewitt served in the navy from three weeks before Pearl Harbor was attacked until almost three months after the war ended. He was on the battleship USS *Indiana* until October 1944, took a 30-day leave (during which he married his wife, Eileen McDaniel in Lewisburg, Virginia) then returned to duty to serve in the Philippine Islands. (Courtesy J. T. Prewitt.)

Charles Ernest Glenn was with the 28th Special Seabee Unit, a branch of the navy founded early in 1942. Seabees usually were work units stationed with the Marine Corps or Army, both on land and on ships. Glenn trained with the Marines at Camp Perry, Virginia. His unit did construction and stevedore (unloading and loading ships) work. Glenn left from Virginia to go to Camp Hueneme, California, one of the largest embarkation points for Seabees headed to the South Pacific. (Courtesy Charles Glenn.)

Telephone lineman Carl Hill (left) and an unidentified serviceman, both probably with the Army's 8430th Signal Service Battalion, string telephone lines along the 1,600-mile Alaskan Highway. Construction began in March 1942 with 11,000 troops and 7,500 civilians. Some men, like George W. Combs Jr. (see page 118), were given permission by their draft boards to go to Alaska to work on this and other military projects as civilians. The Japanese invaded Alaska's Aleutian Islands in June 1942. The highway was completed in September 1942 and became a supply route to bases in Alaska throughout the war. (Courtesy Ollie Collett.)

T5g. Carl Hill of Paint Lick (on top of the bulldozer) and an unidentified crew were slowed down considerably by the dense sub-arctic forest. Once the trees were removed, another hazard presented itself because the frozen ground thawed and became soggy when the layer of permafrost underneath melted into a black sludge. (Courtesy Ollie Collett.)

Carl Hill served in Canada and Alaska. Because wolves were such a threat to the troops, the government put a bounty on them. Here is Hill with several pelts from wolves he killed. (Courtesy Ollie Collett.)

31

Capt. William R. Layton was trained at an officer's candidate school in Nebraska. He was stationed in the Panama Canal Zone and in Peru and Ecuador, with nine long months on the Galapagos Islands where he worked every day around the clock except for sleeping. There was a U.S. Army Air Force base in the Galapogos to protect the Panama Canal Zone, the quickest route for ships traveling from the Atlantic to the Pacific and back. (Courtesy David and Frances Layton.)

Also in the Panama Canal Zone was Eugene Finley of Paint Lick, shown here in Guatemala. He, too, served in the Galapagos Islands. (Courtesy Eugene and Rita Finley.)

Sgt. Robert Guyn of the Army Air Force was stationed at Keesler Air Force Base in Biloxi, Mississippi, when an officer asked for volunteers on a top-secret mission. Bored with where he was, he opted for adventure and volunteered, but he wound up in Peru for the rest of the war at a much slower pace than he anticipated. (Courtesy Lynn Murphy.)

While in Peru, Sgt. Robert Guyn, who had worked at the Peoples Bank in Paint Lick before the war, volunteered again. This time it was to run the post exchange (PX) for the men stationed on the base. These dogs were his faithful companions. (Courtesy Lynn Murphy.)

Forest Bryant, of the Cartersville Road area, was inducted into the army on November 19, 1942. He served as a guard on a navy ship in the Asiatic Pacific theater and crossed the Pacific several times on a cargo ship running supplies back and forth to the troops. (Courtesy Geneva Harrison.)

T5g. William Starnes of Flatwoods trained at Camp Haan, California, for the Army Air Force. "He was in the desert out there and the sun was burning him up," his brother, Paul, recalled. Later he was stationed in the South Pacific and was involved in the taking of the island of Okinawa. (Courtesy Paul and Helen Starnes.)

Sgt. Jack Zanone of Lancaster served in the Army Air Force's Air Transport Command for 30 months at Tezpur in northwestern India. His job was to service planes that "flew the hump" across the Himalaya Mountains, hauling supplies to allied forces in China. (Courtesy Wes Zanone.)

Also stationed in India, Cpl. James Hogan Arnold served at Tezgaon with the 1346th Army Air Force base unit's Air Transport Command. He was inducted in November 1942. Three of his brothers—Andrew, Cecil, and Pete—also served during World War II. A brother-in-law, Hobart Spires, was killed in action during the war. (Courtesy Pete Arnold.)

Most if not all of the crew members in the photograph above were missing and declared dead after contact with their plane was lost, including Gordon Wilson of Buena Vista (first row, second from left). For more information on some of this flight crew, see page 115. Luckier was 1st Lt. James Rankin, at left, who had to force crash land his B-25 Mitchell into the central Pacific Ocean on January 24, 1944, after bombing an objective in the Marshall Islands. After the crash, he and his crew spent 22 hours floating in a raft before being rescued by a PBY flying boat. His back was broken as a result of the crash. Rankin, who flew for the 7th Air Force, had graduated from the Army Air Force Advanced Flying School at Kelly Field in Texas on November 10, 1942. (Courtesy Paul Wilson family, above, and Jim Rankin, left.)

Crossing the equator was a major cause for celebration on most ships. The Marines on the USS *General E. T. Collins* (AP-147), above, held a special "crossing the line" initiation ceremony on board, said Roy Patterson, who served on this ship. The initiate sat on a hinged chair for a haircut. A razor, rigged to shock him, would cause him to fall backward into a vat of ocean water. (Courtesy Roy Patterson.)

Capt. Gilbert "Gib" Wilson was in his third year at Eastern Kentucky State Teachers College in Richmond with the Reserve Officers' Training Corps (ROTC) when he was sent to Officers' Candidacy School at Fort Sill, Oklahoma, where he was commissioned a first lieutenant. He was stationed as a pier officer in the Philippine Islands from 1945 to 1946. He served in the Army for 42 months. (Courtesy Ruth McElveen; information Elvaree Wilson.)

Albin Combs, of the Cartersville Road area, was an electrician on the USS *Terror*, a mine sweeper/layer, from 1943 to 1945. On May 1, 1945, a Japanese kamikaze (suicide bomber) hit the sick bay of the ship. Combs was hit in the head by shrapnel and trapped. The crew, which couldn't reach him yet, asked if he could restore power forward from where he was trapped. He did so in minutes. Many of the soldiers and sailors in sick bay had been killed in the attack. (Courtesy William Combs.)

Toward the end of the war and into the occupation period, Lewis Denver Wilson, of Buena Vista, served on Mine Sweeper 128 in the Pacific from the Aleutian Islands, Alaska, to San Diego, California. On one occasion, shipmates were ordered to board a Russian freighter that had failed to give the correct password. The ship was found to be hauling a legal shipment. (Courtesy Paul Wilson family.)

Cpl. Claude Preston of the army carved his wife's address on a coconut and mailed it home. She received the unusual "letter." While serving at Guadalcanal, Preston saw fellow Garrard Countian Claude Edward Montgomery, a Marine, in the chow line. He would later learn that Montgomery had been killed in fighting the next day. (Courtesy Ron Goens.)

While the history books don't support the story, Cpl. Claude Preston said the army had secured Guadalcanal before the Marines arrived, which might explain why they got little resistance when first landing. Here the Marine Corps films a movie about the taking of Guadalcanal. (Courtesy Ron Goens.)

Members of the crew of the Landing Craft Infantry (LCI) 740, which was at the Marshall Islands, Caroline Islands, and Iwo Jima, pose for a commemorative photograph. The man to the left of the seven in the ship's identification number (with an asterisk above his head) is Samuel Hudson Wilson of Buena Vista, an electrician's mate third class. (Courtesy Paul Wilson family.)

Hudson Wilson's LCI-740 (above) was hit by a kamikaze plane, which took out its radar. The men on the ship divided up mementos from the Japanese plane's wreckage and Wilson was given this photograph as a souvenir. Another time, the ship was anchored off one of the Marshall Islands controlled by the Japanese. The men on board had to stand watch constantly because the Japanese were swimming out and trying to board the ship by climbing the anchor chain. (Courtesy Paul Wilson family.)

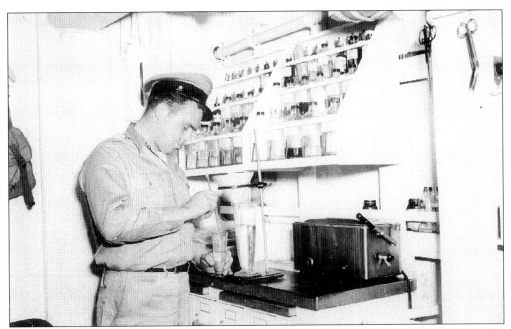

Chief Pharmacist's Mate Nelson Tudor worked in the pharmacy of LST-473. During the September 4, 1943, assault on Lae, New Guinea, his ship and nine others were attacked by 12 Japanese torpedo planes and 15 dive bombers. Tudor died in 2005. A former shipmate wrote Tudor's widow, Christine, after his death: "I can still see him on that deck tending to the wounded and removing the dead." (Courtesy Christine Tudor.)

Robert Rich served on the USS *Sarpedon*, an LST (Landing Ship, Tank) converted to an Auxiliary Repair Battleship (ARB-7). The ship arrived at Okinawa on August 6, 1945, the day Hiroshima was bombed. The ship at anchor next to his was bombed. His own ship took a pounding from nature, enduring two typhoons and a tidal wave. One typhoon sank numerous craft anchored near the *Sarpedon*. For weeks afterward, he saw bodies floating to the surface from the sunken ships. The *Sarpedon* was among the first ships in the Shanghai, China, occupational forces. (Courtesy Norma Rich.)

S.Sgt. Lincoln Harvey Creech of Lancaster was a heavy-motor crewman with the army's 149th Infantry, 38th Division. He was responsible for 17 men whose duties were to set up, aim, and fire weapons from ground mounts to place explosives, toxic gas, shells, or smoke on enemy positions. He was in many battles in the South Pacific, including Bataan, Zig-Zag Pass, Corregidor, and others. (Courtesy Margaret Burkett; information J. C. and Reva Broaddus.)

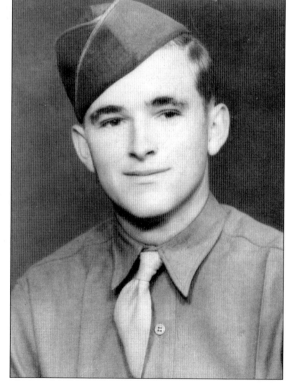

S.Sgt. Bluford E. Sebastian of Nina enlisted in the army in April 1943 and was squad leader for Headquarters Company, 3rd Battalion, 169th Regimental Combat Team of the 43rd "Red Wing" Division in the Southwest Pacific. He saw action in New Guinea, the Northern Solomon Islands, and the liberation of the Philippines, and served a short time in the occupation of Japan. (Courtesy family of Bluford Sebastian.)

Most of the troops in New Guinea lived in huts like the one at right at best, but Pfc. Dan Ledford (standing on left) built this house for himself and his housemates John Cummings, shown here, and Manuel "Big Stoop" Estupian. Netting surrounded the house, so when inside they could roam without being confined to mosquito-netted bunks. (Courtesy Dan Ledford.)

Pfc. Dan Ledford (front, center) befriended some of the New Guinea people near the base. In this photograph, taken September 16, 1944, from left to right are (first row) Rastus, Ledford, and unidentified; (second row) unidentified, Naya (with cup), two unidentified locals, and Manawa. Dan taught Naya to sing the wartime hit "Shoo, Shoo Baby." But Naya pronounced the words, "Soo, Soo, Baby. Don' cy, baby. Your papa off to the seven seas." (Courtesy Dan Ledford.)

At Lae, New Guinea, the scene of earlier fierce fighting, Army Air Force soldiers pose at a Liberty ship that has been bombed by the Japanese. Shown here are, from left to right, (first row) ? Underwood; (second row) ? Zimmerman, ? Huffnagle, Dan Ledford, Alfred Geralds, and John Cummings; (third row) two unidentified soldiers. (Courtesy Dan Ledford.)

Signalman Third Class Eugene Pollard was the only one of five brothers serving in World War II who chose the navy. He boarded a ship in Boston and sailed through the Panama Canal to New Guinea. He was at the invasions of the Philippines, Iwo Jima, and Okinawa, serving on LCI-660, which landed troops for these battles. (Courtesy Eugene Pollard.)

Wilbert Preston (front row, far left), a Seabee, was on the Bataan Peninsula in April 1942, when it fell to the Japanese. He hid out in a cave, using his knife to kill the Japanese who had been in the cave. By doing so, he escaped being part of the Bataan Death March, during which thousands of POWs were marched 100 miles to a prison camp. Along the way, all were starved and tortured, and many of them died or were killed. (Courtesy Ron Goens.)

Y2c. Quentin Earcel Metcalf served on the *Charles J. Kimmel*, Destroyer Escort 584. He was in the service from 1943 through 1946 and was involved in the liberation of the Philippines. (Courtesy Robin and Wendell Metcalf.)

T.Sgt. James Henry Ramsey of Camp Dick flew Consolidated B-24 Liberators for the Army Air Force. In an August 24, 1944, *Central Record* article, he was awarded the Air Medal for courageous service during a long-range reconnaissance mission near Biak Island in which the flight crew encountered 12 Japanese Zero fighters. In the ensuing engagement, the enemy planes damaged three of the bomber's engines and did other extensive damage. The B-24 shot down three of the Zeros and probably destroyed a fourth. (Courtesy Maryann Alquist, above, and Janie Miller, left.)

Once Leyte Island had been taken, the Bataan Peninsula was cut off, which led to the downfall of Manila. Pvt. Woods Walker Lear of Cartersville died in the battle for the island. Here many troops are boarding a ship to be sent to Okinawa, the last major campaign of the war in the Pacific. (Courtesy Roy Patterson.)

Throughout the Pacific, especially in the islands historically occupied by Japan, the Japanese positioned themselves in caves, creating nearly impenetrable pillboxes like this one on Okinawa. Many lives were lost in the battles to gain control of these islands. (Courtesy Roy Patterson.)

Here troops are being loaded onto a ship at Okinawa after that island was taken. During the battle for this island, the famed war correspondent Ernie Pyle was killed. (Courtesy Roy Patterson.)

While on a water run on the Bataan Peninsula in the Philippines in 1945, Pfc. Dan Ledford (not pictured) came upon these two Japanese soldiers (center) who promptly surrendered to him. Using hand signals, he tried to determine where their guns were. They indicated that they had thrown them away. Below is a group of Japanese prisoners taken on the island of Guam also in 1945. (Courtesy Dan Ledford, above, and Roy Patterson, below.)

S1c. Carl Adkison, far left, served as a barber on the USS *Constellation*. He was at the Battle of Luzon Island, Philippines. The other men are not identified. (Courtesy Doan and Mary Adkison.)

Sgt. Frank Starnes was a cook in the 113th Medical Battalion and prepared special diets for patients receiving treatment during the Battle of Zig-Zag Pass on Bataan, Luzon Island, Philippines. He was cited for excellent work and his endurance, which made it possible for him to stay on duty many long hours a day. Before arriving at the Philippines, he served overseas in Hawaii and New Guinea. (Courtesy Geneva Starnes.)

S1c. Letcher Wildes "Buddy" Christopher Jr. (below left) served on LST-72 and marked his gun position in this photograph. Prior to his enlistment on August 9, 1944, this ship participated in the Normandy invasion from June 6 to 25, 1944. Christopher served in the navy until February 25, 1946. After the fighting in Europe ended, the ship was sent to the Pacific, where it remained during the occupation period. (Courtesy Paula Hatfield.)

(*Above right*) In the spring of 1945, Lt. John Frank Conn of the Army Air Force had a harrowing experience while flying a B-29 Superfortress over Japan. A Japanese machine-gun bullet entered the nose of the plane and severed a hydraulic line, spraying the sticky red fluid onto the inside of the windshield. "We actually were flying blind for a while," he recounted in a *Central Record* article published April 26, 1945. (Courtesy Mitzi Makenas.)

Fighting in the Pacific took its toll on soldiers. Notice the difference in stance and expression at Batangos, Luzon Island, in the Philippines, between replacement troop Elmore Green (left) and Frank Vinson, who had seen combat. (Courtesy Lorene Green and Jim Drake.)

Three

ATLANTIC, EUROPEAN, AND NORTH AFRICAN THEATER

In World War I and later in the 1930s, the Germans erected and fortified this barrier opposite the French Maginot Line to impede an invasion of Germany. The Germans called it the West Wall; the Americans, the Siegfried Line. Here near Christmas 1944, Sgt. Walter Lee "Pete" Arnold (left) and Sgt. Robert Furman pose after the Germans retreated under Allied pressure. (Courtesy Pete Arnold.)

The *Queen Mary* luxury liner was converted into a troop transport ship during the war. Pfc. John M. Adkison, of Hackley, crossed the Atlantic in October 1942 on the ship's second voyage as such. Off the coast of Ireland, she rammed another ship, the British cruiser *Curacao*, cutting the latter in half and killing 338 of the men on board. Under orders not to stop for anything, the *Queen Mary* continued toward England. (Courtesy Doan and Mary Adkison.)

In a V-Mail letter (see an example on page 62) published April 15, 1943, in the *Central Record*, Pfc. Charles Zanone of Lancaster wrote that in North Africa candy bars cost 20¢, beer 45¢, and no cigars were available. He said he would rather be sitting in at another session at Lancaster hangout Cole Drug to talk about everything from baseball to how the war was progressing. (Courtesy Wes Zanone.)

Cpl. Harold Ralston is pictured here in Casablanca, Morocco. In a September 20, 1943, letter to his uncle, he wrote: "Exactly three months ago today, I saw what I had looked for for several days—land! I shall never forget that sight—just an outline of something between the ocean and the sky. Africa, for the first time showing up through the moonlight." (Courtesy Harold Ralston.)

S.Sgt. Robert Murphy of Lancaster poses with some natives selling grapes in North Africa. He and his brother, Waddell, had not seen each other since the beginning of the war. The Red Cross arranged for them to meet in Naples, Italy, where Waddell's ship was in port. They flew Robert in, but the plane's landing gear wouldn't come down. By the time the problem was fixed, Waddell's ship had sailed. (Courtesy Donna Powell.)

The staging area in the southern port of Marseille, France, en route from Naples, Italy, to Nancy, France, is where many soldiers were pulled with overnight notice to help replace the heavy losses at the Battle of the Bulge in Belgium. (Courtesy Harold Ralston.)

Cpl. Harold Ralston writes a letter home during a lull. In his September 20, 1943, letter (published in the *Central Record* October 14, 1943), he said he had received a letter from Sgt. Robert Guyn, also of Paint Lick, and wondered how school pals Gilbert Wilson and the Moore boys were doing. He also guessed at what was being done on the farm with the tobacco and corn crops. (Courtesy Harold Ralston.)

Four G.I.s on a three-day Rest and Relaxation (R and R) tour of Florence, Italy, in 1944 pose in front of the cathedral. From left to right, they are J. B. Tolison, unidentified, Lt. (jg) Manford Waddell Murphy, and unidentified. (Courtesy Donna Powell.)

First Lt. Wilton C. Teater poses with his Virginia bride, Myra Dorsett, on their September 4, 1943, wedding day, in Petersburg, Virginia, just before he went overseas. Teater had served since July 27, 1940, in the Army Armored Force, founded about two weeks before. "I can truthfully say that I have grown up with Uncle Sam's 'panzer' division," he wrote in a letter in the *Central Record* December 18, 1941, comparing his U.S. tank division to the panzer one in Germany. (Courtesy Harold Ralston.)

One of the many African Americans from Garrard County who served, Arthur Dunn of Boones Creek was with the 92nd Division's field artillery in Italy, France, and Belgium. He remembers befriending some of the starving children of Italy. He used to fill a plate of food and give it to a young brother and sister. Then he would wash the plate and get his own chow. Below, Dunn returned to Europe in the 1960s and visited this U.S. military cemetery in France where many of America's fallen heroes were buried. (Courtesy Arthur and Mary Dunn.)

Above, Sgt. Leslie Coy Dyehouse (left), who has just been presented with a Bronze Star, is congratulated by Maj. Gen. Geoffrey Keyes on June 20, 1944, in Rome, Italy. Dyehouse, of the Crab Orchard postal route, was an MP (military police) with Headquarters 11 Corps. He received this honor for heroic action on January 2, 1944, in the vicinity of Mignano, Italy, where he and several men in his unit came to the aid of five men seriously wounded by a shell that exploded nearby, despite the threat of continued shelling. At right, Dyehouse poses with the daughter of the woman hired to do laundry for Dyehouse and others in the camp. (Courtesy Inez Dyehouse.)

Some troops gathered and trained in England for at least a year awaiting the invasion of continental Europe. Above, Bradley Green (far left) of Cartersville and two unidentified buddies enjoy some R and R in an outdoor cafe. Green wrote home to tell his mother he was in England and had met a fellow Garrard Countian, Pfc. John Milton Adkison, at left, who "was looking fine." Adkison, a member of the 111th Field Artillery Batallion of the 29th Infantry Division, was in the first wave to hit Omaha Beach in Normandy, France, on June 6, 1944. Green also was involved in the invasion on Omaha Beach, which had the highest casualties of any beach on D-Day. Adkison survived and was discharged in May 1945. Green also survived D-Day and subsequent battle campaigns. (Courtesy Doan and Mary Adkison.)

Nathan Prewitt fought with the 1st Battalion, 29th Infantry in the Normandy, Northern France, Rhineland, and Central Europe campaigns. He was wounded in France on August 8, 1944, and in Germany on November 17, 1944. (Courtesy Susie Vasquez.)

This is the soldier who sent his sweetheart the postcard shown on page 11 from Camp Shelby near Hattiesburg, Mississippi. While a man of few words, he did win the girl, Allene Conn, and was married February 2, 1946. (Courtesy Susie Vasquez.)

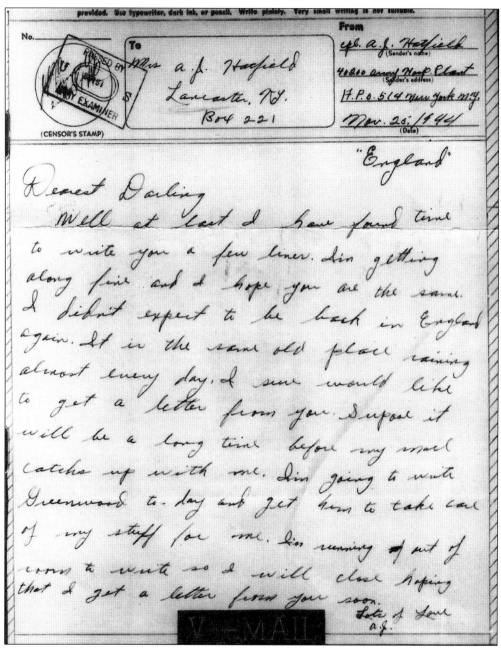

Cpl. A. J. Hatfield wrote this November 25, 1944, V-Mail letter to his wife, Lorraine, from England. During the latter years of World War II, V-Mail became a popular way to correspond with a loved one serving overseas. It consisted of miniaturized messages reproduced by microphotography from 16-mm film. As with regular mail, it still was censored to make sure no military secrets were revealed inadvertently. When he wrote this letter, Hatfield had been injured and sent to a hospital in England. Eventually, he was able to return to the Anti-Tank Company of the 394th Infantry for the Rhineland campaign into Germany. (Courtesy Lorraine Hatfield.)

Cpl. A. J. Hatfield was inducted on December 17, 1942, and took basic training in Macon, Georgia. He trained to drive and repair light and heavy trucks. Hatfield was stationed in North Africa at the time of the invasion of Sicily. Afterward he was shipped to England for the Normandy invasion and the Northern France campaign. He was wounded November 18, 1944. (Courtesy Lorraine Hatfield.)

Pfc. John M. Adkison of Paint Lick is pictured here with his 105-mm Howitzer light artillery. He fought with Battery A, 880th Field Artillery Battalion and was in the battles of Normandy, Northern France, Rhineland, and Central Europe. (Courtesy Doan and Mary Adkison.)

T.Sgt. Ralph Starnes, of Paint Lick, was an engineer-gunner in B-17 Flying Fortress and B-24 Liberator bombers with the 486th Bombardier Group, 3rd Air Division. He flew with the same crew for 30 missions over Germany, each time returning safe and unharmed. (Courtesy Ralph and Thelma Starnes.)

J. W. Teater went into service on April 30, 1942, and served 38 months and 11 days overseas in England, France, and Africa. He was with the 8th Air Force, 92nd Bombardier Group, 327th Squadron. He returned to the states on the *Queen Mary* and was discharged October 23, 1945. "The only good thing I can say about my time overseas was that I made it through," Teater told Margaret Burkett in 2005. (Courtesy Peggy Derringer.)

Bradley Green landed at Omaha Beach in Normandy on D-Day, and his unit survived to make its way into Germany. In France, he wrote home: "I think we have been doing alright here in France. I take my helmet and find a cow and get the hat full of milk. I have a little trouble getting them to stand still sometimes. I don't think they understand my language. The helmet sure is a handy thing to have around. I use it to shave, take a bath, wash my feet, and as a milk bucket. The rest of the time I wear it. I get along fine with the French people, what few I have seen. Of course I can't talk much to them, I just have to make signs." (Courtesy Ella Green.)

John W. Vaskuhl (left) and Pfc. Clarence J. Hurt served with the medical corps in France in 1945. Hurt is from Back Creek and trained at Camp Butner in North Carolina with Company C of the 92nd Medical Battalion. Hurt drove the trucks that transported the wounded to the medical tents and hauled supplies to the front. (Courtesy Barbara Todd.)

Two Paint Lick men who were wounded in Europe are Frank Clay "Scraper" Dillon, left, and Woodford Bowling, shown back at home in Paint Lick on medical leave in 1945. Dillon suffered from frostbite in the Battle of the Bulge. Bowling was injured in Germany on March 4, 1945, during the Rhineland campaign. Within nine days of crossing the Saar River, his company in the 417th Infantry had gone from about 130 men down to nine. The rest had been killed or wounded. (Courtesy Woodford Bowling.)

James R. Adams, of Buckeye, lost two Christmases while in service. Drafted in December 1942, he reached Camp Wheeler, Georgia, a few days before Christmas but was restricted to the barracks. In 1944, he was wounded on December 21 in the Northern France campaign and spent seven days unconscious following surgeries to remove shrapnel. (Courtesy Barry Adams.)

Franklin Tramuel Wilson, of Paint Lick, joined the navy in September 1940 and was aboard the USS *Augusta* on August 9, 1941, four months before Pearl Harbor was attacked, when Pres. Franklin Roosevelt held a clandestine conference with Prime Minister Winston Churchill off the coast of Newfoundland. This summit produced a strategy for fighting World War II that helped solidify the Allies to eventually prevail over the Axis powers. (Courtesy Ruth McElveen.)

S.Sgt. Eugene Preston of Mount Hebron was in the medical detachment of an Armored Field Artillery Battalion. While in the vicinity of Wehingen, Germany, he crawled several hundred yards to reach wounded soldiers and render first aid. Then seeing that a truck had received a direct hit and was blocking the roadway, he mounted another truck amidst a hail of shell fire and used it to push the damaged vehicle off the road. (Courtesy Ron Goens.)

According to a letter written April 25, 1945, to his foster sister, Nellie Ray, in Bryantsville, Pfc. James Grimes was in Thayer Army Hospital in Nashville. Grimes, of Sugar Creek, was being treated for wounds received December 31, 1944, and January 2, 1945, in Belgium. (Courtesy Brenda Eason.)

These three brothers from the Back Creek area served in World War II. Pfc. William Harry Turner (above, left) served from 1943 to 1946. He was a railway powerman with the army's 723rd Railway Operations Battalion and was in the Northern France, Rhineland, and Central Europe campaigns. James Richard Turner (above, right) served with the army in Italy and Czechoslovakia. Pvt. Boyd Benton Turner (below, right), who also served with the army, was wounded in the European theater of operations and received a Purple Heart. (Courtesy Janice Amon.)

Pfc. Andrew Roy Arnold, of Bryantsville, trained with a tank division before joining the 95th Infantry Division, where he served in Europe. He was wounded in late 1944 in France. His brother, Pete, serving nearby, tried to visit him in Luxembourg, but Andrew had not yet been released from the hospital. "It was a wonder I ever found his division," Pete Arnold said. "I guess I learned to read a map real well." (Courtesy Pete Arnold.)

George R. Tudor of Paint Lick served as a military policeman in the army from 1943 to 1946. He was wounded in Germany and hospitalized in Italy for 22 months. (Courtesy Betty Tudor.)

These four Kentucky nurses, above, joined the Army Air Force to serve their country and help ease suffering. From left to right are M. Champlin, Blanche Montgomery, and sisters from western Kentucky, Mary and Lillian Chapman. Serving with the 317th Station Hospital in England, in addition to carrying out their nursing duties, they spent time talking to patients about things of interest to the men and bringing to them a home-like atmosphere. First Lt. Montgomery (right) was stationed in Northern Ireland and England in early 1944. On August 15, 1944, she accepted a temporary assignment at an undisclosed location in Europe and was issued combat clothing and equipment. In April 1945, the unit arrived in Normandy as the war drew to a close. (Courtesy Wilma Cornelius.)

Cpl. Paul Starnes, left, was with the 329th Infantry Regiment, 83rd Infantry Division, and first saw combat at St. Malo, France. Sometime after the taking of the citadel there, his regiment found itself on the banks of this river (below). Starnes guarded this bridge for six days, sleeping in a nearby hotel when off duty. Before the Allies could cross it though, the Germans blew up the middle section of the bridge. The Germans surrendered once they knew it was the Americans and not the French who would be capturing them. (Courtesy Paul and Helen Starnes.)

Pfc. Elmer "Hot Shot" Wilmot (right) is photographed with an unidentified buddy. Wilmot trained at Anniston, Alabama, and was sent to Germany, where his regiment went in and secured towns, making sure no enemy soldiers were hiding after the Allies had taken the towns. (Photograph courtesy Rhonda Ellis; information Phyllis Hicks.)

Pfc. Elmer "Hot Shot" Wilmot spent nine months of his almost 17 months of service as a light truck driver. He served with the 115th Field Artillery Battalion in the European theater of operations, transporting personnel, equipment, and supplies. (Courtesy Phyllis Hicks.)

Sgt. Walter L. "Pete" Arnold stands next to one of the German pillbox defenses taken out along the Siegfried Line. He wrote in his memoirs, "We set up three guns—two 57-mm and a 76. We pounded and we pounded and we pounded, hitting the same spot. . . . After I had fired 100 rounds with my 57-mm Anti-Tank gun, we finally broke through." (Courtesy Pete Arnold.)

Just before the war ended in Europe, word came of the sudden death of Pres. Franklin D. Roosevelt. Harold Ralston writes that this photograph is of his Army Air Force unit's Roosevelt memorial formation in Nancy, France. (Courtesy Harold Ralston.)

Four

KEEPING THE
HOME FIRES BURNING

Even before America had entered the war, Garrard Countians were helping to support those in Great Britain under bombardment from Germany. In the spring of 1941, Lancaster High School home economics students like this girl made 20 baby layette sets in the "Bundles for Britain" relief effort. In the summer of 1944, Anna Broaddus, one of the students, received a letter from a British mother saying she had just received the layette—baby clothes and blankets—made by Broaddus and was delighted with them. (Courtesy Garrard County Jail Museum.)

The Selective Service Draft was reinstituted in 1940. Bascom Ford, who later would be killed in Italy, volunteered to join up even before his number was drawn. Here a group of Garrard County men check the draft numbers outside the courthouse in 1940. Identified are Cleo Dollins (far left), Bud Oakes (plaid jacket), Herbert Adams (in overalls), and J. Travis Hume (on steps, far right). Ross Bastin and Billy Mason are also in the photo. (Courtesy Garrard County Jail Museum.)

Residents of Lancaster and Garrard County gathered in front of the courthouse on Public Square for a war-bond drawing. As a result of sales in 1943, the USS *Garrard* (see chapter five) would be commissioned in 1945 and named for the county. (Courtesy Lynn Murphy.)

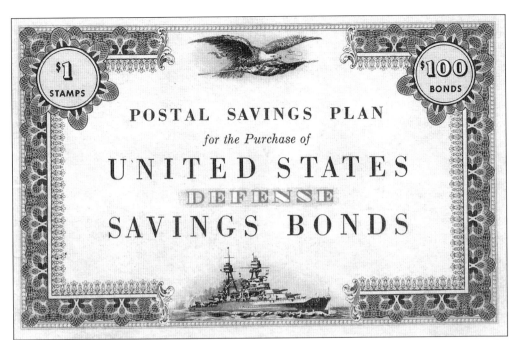

U.S. Defense Savings Bonds booklets were put out by the post office and made it easier for people to purchase bonds in smaller increments. In the case of this one, patrons paid $1 for each stamp and affixed each one on pages like the one below. When they had filled the booklet, they would bring it to the post office and redeem it for a bond. In the short-run, the bonds would help fund the war effort. In later years, bond owners could cash them in with interest. (Courtesy Jerome Layton via the Garrard County Jail Museum.)

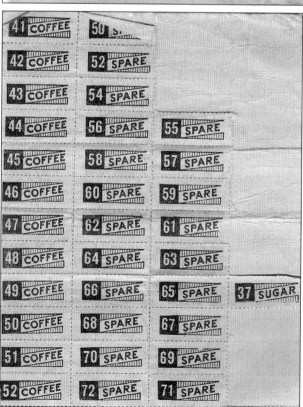

UNITED STATES OF AMERICA
OFFICE OF PRICE ADMINISTRATION

795 086   **AD**

WAR RATION BOOK No. 3

Void if altered

NOT VALID WITHOUT STAMP

Identification of person to whom issued: PRINT IN FULL

Doris   H.   Barker

(First name)   (Middle name)   (Last name)

Street number or rural route _Route 4_

City or post office _Lancaster_   State _Ky_

AGE	SEX	WEIGHT	HEIGHT	OCCUPATION
11	Female	80 Lbs.	4 Ft. 3 In.	

SIGNATURE _____
(Person to whom book is issued. If such person is unable to sign because of age or incapacity, another may sign in his behalf.)

WARNING

This book is the property of the United States Government. It is unlawful to sell it to any other person, or to use it or permit anyone else to use it, except to obtain rationed goods in accordance with regulations of the Office of Price Administration. Any person who finds a lost War Ration Book must return it to the War Price and Rationing Board which issued it. Persons who violate rationing regulations are subject to $10,000 fine or imprisonment, or both.

OPA Form No. R-130

LOCAL BOARD ACTION

Issued by _____
(Local board number)   (Date)

Street address _____

City _____   State _____

(Signature of issuing officer)

To boost production and maintain supply levels for troops abroad, Americans at home were asked to conserve materials and to use ration stamps to limit the amount of certain products they bought or used, including gasoline, rubber, shoes, coffee, sugar, butter, and some kinds of cloth. Above is 11-year-old Doris Barker's War Ration Book 3. At left is an example of ration stamps from late in the war. To aid the public and control distribution of scarce items, newspapers published a daily "Ration Calendar" telling the current status of many goods at the local level: "Last day to use Coffee 41 stamp" or "Spare 52 stamp must accompany application for additional canning from rationing boards." (Courtesy Doris Baker via the Garrard County Jail Museum, above, and Paul Wilson family, left.)

Maxine Foresler "Mom" Blakeman owned the Southern Kitchen in Lancaster, but she almost had to close down during the war because her sales receipts didn't warrant enough food points to stock her restaurant. The government checked to see how many meals she served and learned she let all non-commissioned servicemen eat free. She was given the points she needed to continue. (Courtesy Mom Blakeman's Candy, Inc.)

These Lancaster ladies held a party for some soldiers passing through from outside Garrard County on June 20, 1942. This image includes servicemen Raymond Heft, James Durham, William Schroeder, Joe Neilson, John Brosseau, Elbert Powell, John Cosgrove, Bill Bess, Orville Zeller, Bill Nickell, and Tom McDyer. The ladies are Anna Miller, Mary Ruth Winburn, Anne Engle, Anna Zanone, Dolly Sanders, Doris Wood, Mable Thompson, and Jane Elliott. The order is unknown. (Courtesy Lynn Murphy.)

In August 1941, an ill young army officer and his wife were trying to get to a Dayton base from one in Louisiana. He had encountered indifference to his plight during the trip. In Lancaster, druggist Ben Wood (left), a World War I veteran, let him use his phone and then made arrangements to remove him by ambulance to the hospital at Fort Thomas, Kentucky; the soldier sent a thank-you letter in 1942 with some money to help pay the phone-call costs. Also in photograph is Ben's wife, Jennie. (Courtesy Betty Wood.)

In late 1943, their son, Thomas Benjamin Wood, joined the navy's new program for 17-year-olds. A fall down some steps resulted in a broken arm that needed to be rebroken and reset when it did not heal, preventing him from completing that program. He later became a navy fireman second class. Here he is on Danville Road outside Lancaster after marrying Betty Jo Arnold on April 12, 1946. The newlyweds were on their way to Louisville for a one-night honeymoon. After-war gas rationing prohibited them from going any farther. (Courtesy Betty Wood.)

Visits home during and after the war lifted the spirits of the folks at home as much as those of the servicemen. Pictured here from left to right, Harold Ralston; his father, Robert Frank Sr; and brother, Robert Frank Jr., share a visit in Paint Lick. (Courtesy Harold Ralston.)

The Mallie and John Rich (second row, far right) family on Fall Lick Road also had two sons in the war effort (Walter, first row, center, and Robert first row, far right). Daughter Edna (second row, second from left) did her part by driving ammunitions trucks at Camp Atterbury in Indiana on rough roads and often late at night. (Courtesy Lucille Rich and Betty Norment.)

Some women went into the ordnance depots and factories to support the war effort. From 1943 to 1945, navy wife Dorothy Baierlein worked at the Lyon Electric Plant in San Diego near the base where her Lancaster-native husband, Henry, was stationed. She usually made resistors for bombers but is working on a drill press in this photograph. (Courtesy Dorothy Lynch.)

Mary Frances "Frankie" Tudor of Paint Lick worked at the Blue Grass Army Ordnance Depot in Richmond during the later war years. In January 1946, she left for New York City to attend the Navy WAVES Training School along with four Madison County girlfriends who also had worked at the depot. (Courtesy Betty Tudor.)

Some wives followed servicemen to basic and advanced training camps. Here Dorothy and Henry Baierlein pose in front of their San Diego home on June 7, 1943, their second wedding anniversary. He was stationed at the North Island Naval Center there and shipped out to the South Pacific in October 1944. Originally from Oklahoma, Dorothy met Henry on a visit to her cousin, then a minister at First Presbyterian Church in Lancaster. (Courtesy Dorothy Lynch.)

Elmore Green's Cartersville family was taken in by a woman in Hattiesburg, Mississippi, near Camp Shelby. From left to right in this cotton field are his mother, Jennie Green, who was visiting; Elmore; his wife, Lorene; the Greens' baby son, James, being held by an unidentified tenant farmer; and Lillie Ware, the woman who hosted the Greens. (Courtesy Lorene Green and Jim Drake.)

In June 1943, before he was inducted into active duty, schoolteacher Glenmore Cotton wrote to his brother, Ralph, already in service, about progress on the farm. Garrard County families had to help each other out with so many men off to war, as indicated in his letter: "I am going to help Owsley and Bud set tobacco tomorrow. We got their corn planted last week. . . . Barnes has set his tobacco out once. I helped him set it and he helped me plant corn." (Courtesy Sharon Hamilton.)

J. C. Rogers, left (saluting), and Pvt. Ralph H. Cotton, both of Garrard County, share some non–army issue transportation. Cotton entered the army on September 25, 1942, and was sent to Camp Backley, Texas, where he was assigned to a medical detail. Not long after he returned to the farm, his brother, Glenmore (above) was inducted. (Courtesy Sharon Hamilton; information Reba Cotton.)

Walter L. "Pete" Arnold was in Luxembourg when his mother wrote him of the death of his grandmother, Tillie Hagan, pictured here with his grandfather, Robert L. Hagan. The Germans intercepted the letter, along with some cookies. Robert and Tillie had at least five grandsons serving in World War II, one of whom, Robert Francis Jennings, was killed in action, as was their granddaughter's husband, Hobart Spires. (Courtesy Pete Arnold.)

Elmore Green (far left) of Cartersville, on leave from the army, visits with (from left to right) Bradley Combs, Henry Green (his father), and Pierce Allen at Bradley Combs's Garrard County farm. Elmore Green served 11 months in the Pacific in three campaigns. (Courtesy William Combs.)

John Boyle, front and center, is surrounded by family members while on furlough in Lowell. His parents are Oscar and Theressa Brown Boyle, at far left in the second row. His sisters' families, the McWhorters and Millers, also are at the gathering. (Courtesy John Boyle.)

As soldiers, sailors, and Marines returned home from service after the war, there were gatherings of families and neighbors anxious to celebrate and help them begin readjusting to life in Garrard County. Shown here from left to right are Bill Broaddus; Clell Dean Prewitt; Joe Sutton; Veta Frances Sebastian Foley; her husband, Paul R Foley (home from Alaska and the Aleutian Islands); and Russell Sutton, who didn't want to stop eating long enough to pose for this photograph. (Courtesy Darwin Foley.)

Five

USS GARRARD

The USS *Garrard* (APA-84), sitting at anchor in 1945, was an amphibious attack transport ship. Crew members at the 2002 ship's reunion in Garrard County apologized for mispronouncing the name for nearly 60 years. They had always pronounced it the USS Ja-RARD. "We found out for the first time this year you pronounce it GAIR-rid," said shipmate Chuck Hillinger. (Courtesy Ken Billings via Garrard County Jail Museum.)

The USS *Garrard* was commissioned at 1430 hours on March 3, 1945, at Pier 58, Naval Supply Depot, San Pedro, California. Lt. Comdr. Walter Barnett Jr. assumed command of the *Garrard*. More than 23 officers, 236 members of the crew, and 75 members of the boat group, with family members including shipmate Earl Goodwin's wife, Allene (watching from the upper deck), looking on. (Courtesy Earl and Gary Goodwin; information Lt. G. E. Hendricks's brief history.)

Ken Billings (far left) and some unidentified crewmates from the USS *Garrard* enjoy a shore leave, possibly in California. (Courtesy Kenneth Billings and Garrard County Jail Museum.)

The signal corps of the USS *Garrard* before the end of the war consisted of, from left to right, (first row) Clark Drane, Eugene Benson, and Rocco De Nigris; (second row) Charles Hardin and Robby Dyson; (third row) Charles Andrews, Louis McLoney, James Tady, Clarence Jaros, Billie Joe Harp, and Willard Converse; (fourth row) Mike Rhodes, Burton Eppen, Robert Wiedel, and James Durian. (Courtesy Robert Wiedel.)

Signalman Robert Wiedel stands at the signal light on the bridge of the USS *Garrard*. The signalman identified flags from other vessels; was well-versed in the use of blinker, searchlight, and semaphore signals; and used searchlights and signal apparatus like this signal light. During the occupation period after hostilities ended, Wiedel became chief of the USS *Garrard*'s signal crew. (Courtesy Robert Wiedel.)

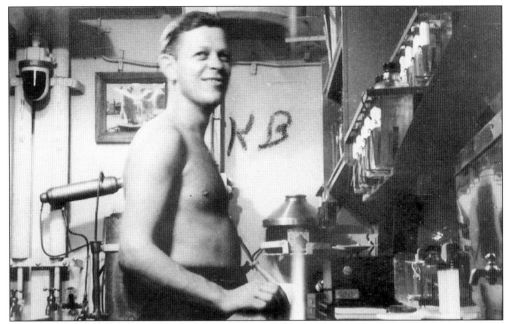

Ken Billings, pharmacist's mate, is seen in the pharmacy on the USS *Garrard*, where he took charge of the sick bay, performed minor surgeries, and administered simple medicines. (Courtesy Ken Billings via Garrard County Jail Museum.)

Ken Billings relaxes on the deck of the USS *Garrard*. The sailing wasn't always this smooth, though. In addition to daily duties, Billings and every crewmember were assigned general quarters positions—the stations to which they would report to prepare for battle. Far less exciting, each crew member also was expected to take a turn on mess cook duty. (Courtesy Ken Billings via Garrard County Jail Museum.)

The USS *Garrard* was part of a Marine landing force created from the Marine complement of all the Third Fleet battleships and carriers. The ship landed some of the first Marines on August 30, 1945, at Yokosuka, Japan, to begin the occupation. In the days to follow, they transported troops back and forth from 10 battleships and 10 aircraft carriers. On September 10, the ship picked up 1,000 former military and civilian POWs at Sendai, Japan, and transported them to Tokyo. (Courtesy Ken Billings via the Garrard County Jail Museum; information Lt. G. E. Hendricks's brief history.)

This is the Yokosuka Naval Base in September 1945. Located just inside Tokyo Bay, it became a strategic embarkation and debarkation point. Today, the U.S. Navy has its most strategic naval facility in the Western Pacific at this location. (Courtesy Ken Billings via Garrard County Jail Museum.)

After the war with Japan ended, the Yokohama Railway Station near Tokyo was used by many of the troops to traverse Japan. They often came through this station on their way to board ships for the trip home from Yokohama, the deep-water port for Tokyo. (Courtesy Ken Billings via Garrard County Jail Museum.)

Shipmate Ken Billings snapped this photograph while on leave in Yokohama, Japan. Results of Allied bombings were evident throughout the city. (Courtesy Ken Billings via Garrard County Jail Museum.)

The USS *Garrard* crew transported homeward-bound troops from the Philippines after the war as part of Operation Magic Carpet to return troops home from Pacific locations. Here in the fall of 1945, some unidentified sailors from the USS *Garrard* pose in front of the ruins of a bombed-out building in Manila. (Courtesy Robert Wiedel.)

Also believed to be in Manila, crewmembers pose in front of what appears to be a presidio in the fall of 1945. In October, the USS *Garrard* returned 726 homeward-bound troops to Portland, Oregon. She then carried out one of Magic Carpet voyages from San Francisco to the Philippines and back, returning in January 1946 with 905 more troops. (Courtesy Robert Wiedel.)

This view shows the bow of the USS *Garrard* at anchor in the Philippines in the fall of 1945. Shipmate Roger E. Kirkpatrick wrote to the author, "I don't know how far we actually traveled during this duty assignment, but my best guess would be over 125,000 miles in anywhere from glass smooth water to waves approaching 100 feet—a ride I will never forget. The USS *Garrard* was a very strong ship true to its namesake and had a crew and officers to match. We all came through a very difficult period standing tall indeed, like the rest of the United States of America." (Courtesy Robert Wiedel.)

Six

WAR ENDS, OCCUPATION BEGINS

Five-star general Dwight D. Eisenhower (left) confers with Col. Daniel Collins Elkin (center), chief of surgery at Ashford General Hospital in White Sulphur Springs, West Virginia, and Col. Alfred Beck in July 1945, after hostilities in Europe had ended. General Eisenhower and his wife, Mamie, were resting at Ashford General Hospital, near the famed Greenbrier Resort. Dr. Elkin was a former Lancaster resident stationed with the army medical corps. In 1949, Elkin became a brigadier general in the army reserves. He retired to Lancaster in later years. (Courtesy Lynn Murphy.)

Edwin Sutton, above, was stationed with the army's quartermaster corps in Greenland (below) during the war and wrote home August 14, 1945: "I hardly know how to write this letter tonight or how to start it. The greatest news in history came tonight, and the burden has at last lifted from every person in the world. . . . I just had to have a big cry tonight. Not because I was sad, but happy." (Courtesy Judy Williams.)

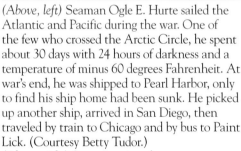

(*Above, left*) Seaman Ogle E. Hurte sailed the Atlantic and Pacific during the war. One of the few who crossed the Arctic Circle, he spent about 30 days with 24 hours of darkness and a temperature of minus 60 degrees Fahrenheit. At war's end, he was shipped to Pearl Harbor, only to find his ship home had been sunk. He picked up another ship, arrived in San Diego, then traveled by train to Chicago and by bus to Paint Lick. (Courtesy Betty Tudor.)

(*Above, right*) Some continued to serve overseas for months, including Sgt. Walter Lee "Pete" Arnold, stationed in Deggendorf, Germany, in July 1945. His unit was preparing to head to the Pacific to invade Japan. "Thank God we never did have to make that trip," wrote Arnold in his memoirs. (Courtesy Pete Arnold.)

(*At right*) Pete's younger brother, Cpl. Cecil Arnold, was among the replacement recruits sent to Germany in 1945. On the ship to Europe, he learned he was to be a military policeman in Germany. Arnold was in one of the honor guards in Heidelberg when Gen. George Patton's casket lay in state after he was killed in a jeep accident. (Courtesy Cecil Arnold.)

Pvt. Carl Rhodus was in Europe for three weeks before being captured by the Germans. Conditions in the prison camp were horrendous. Once when he looked up at an airplane flying overhead, a German soldier struck him, breaking his back. Despite his injury, he was forced to continue working on half rations and less. His weight went from 150 pounds down to 80 pounds. (Courtesy Clellagene Rhodus and sons.)

In a German prison camp, one of the Allied soldier's two dog tags was taken away and replaced with a German one like this one. Here is the one Pvt. Carl Rhodus received, indicating he was prisoner #09 4000 at Stalag XII A (12A). (Courtesy Clellagene Rhodus and sons.)

BANCROFT HOTEL AND ANNEX
COLLINS AVE., MIAMI BEACH, FLORIDA. 2286

Former POW Pvt. Carl Rhodus spent two weeks recuperating at the Bancroft Hotel in Miami Beach, Florida, regaining his strength before being discharged in November 1945. Conley Jennings (below) recuperated at Camp Crowder, Missouri, and was discharged in October 1945. (Courtesy Clellagene Rhodus and sons.)

Conley Jennings was a POW in Stalag 4B in Germany. Most Red Cross boxes were kept from prisoners. Starving, he remembered his mother, Goldie Jennings of Cartersville, picking and cooking greens in the springtime. Prisoners poured their watery soup over the greens for added nutrients. Once they stole an onion from the kitchen and ate it as one would an apple. Many died from diphtheria and starvation before freedom came in May 1945. (Courtesy Connie Brown.)

This officers' mess tent somewhere in Germany shows Charles Baierlein is the back (dark uniform) at far left. None of the others are identified. Notice the pot-bellied stove on the left-hand side, which was used in tents large and small. Only officers were permitted to use this facility. (Courtesy Dorothy Lynch.)

Capt. Charles Baierlein, of Lancaster, was attending the University of Kentucky and in the ROTC when the war broke out. He was able to continue in school for a while then was sent into active service. He was stationed in Germany at the end of the war and during the early occupation period. He later completed his degree and became an architectural engineer. (Courtesy Dorothy Lynch.)

UT GOING		SHIPS IN PORT			UNITS IN CA...		
NAME OF SHIP	TENTATIVE LOADING TIME	NAME	DUE TO SAIL		SHIPMENT NUMBER	UNIT	DATE ARRIVE
		U.S.S. Lyon	2-5 APR				
		Gen Taylor Vic	2-5 APR				
		Montclair Vic	2-5 APR				
		Sea Fiddler	2-5 APR				
		SHIP FORECAST					
		NAME	ESTIMATED TIME ARRIVAL	CAPACITY			
		Frederick Vic	APR 2	1000			
		Ernie Pyle	APR 5	3300			
		Gen Buckner	APR 3	5200		RE-3529 Gisuttes	M 31
SS Lyon 031000		Sea Flier	APR 4	1581	RE-7494 J 92 0 d		31 MA
Frederick V 030700		Blanche Sigman	APR 4	7 ±		d	31 MA
		Chanute Vic	APR 4	1000		d	31 MA
		W.S. Vic	APR 7	1000			
		Maritime Vic	APR 7	1000		NG BN	1 APR
		Westminster Vic	APR 8	1000		T Co	2 APR

Having received his orders to head home, this unidentified soldier checks the schedule board at LeHavre, France, in April 1946 to see when his ship will come in. (Courtesy Jim Schooler.)

The port at LeHavre is familiar to many who served in Europe. From here, thousands of troops shipped out for home. Grover P. Schooler Jr., a technician grade five in the Army Air Force, took these photographs while waiting to sail home on the USS *Lyon*. (Courtesy Jim Schooler.)

U.S. Army Air Force sergeant Robert Frank Ralston Jr. of Paint Lick was privileged to be the crew chief on the aircraft assigned to U.S. Supreme Court justice Robert Jackson, chief council for the United States in the 1945–1946 Nuremberg Nazi war crimes trials. (Courtesy Harold Ralston.)

In the weeks following VE Day, Pfc. Robert L. Tracy (right), of Lancaster (originally from Buckeye) visited with two other Garrard County servicemen in Nuremberg—Pfc. Oneal LeMay of Bryantsville and Tracy's brother, Sgt. William Howard Tracy. The latter had been in service for three years and overseas 21 months and this was the first time he had seen anyone he knew from home. (Courtesy Mike and Phyllis Tracy.)

At war's end, the Advanced Service Rating (ASR) determined when troops would be sent home from the European theater. Based on number of months served, awards received, number of children, and other factors, a score of 85 and higher earned the earliest discharge. Pfc. Wesley Poynter (right) of Paint Lick had fought in the Ardennes, Rhineland, and Central Europe campaigns and won three Bronze Stars. His score was 47. (Courtesy Paul and Helen Starnes.)

As battle troops were sent home, fresh ones were rotated in, including Joel Rollins Sr., who served in Germany from about 1947 to 1949. The United States maintains bases in Germany to this day. (Courtesy Katie Rollins.)

This Christmas greeting card was sent to family in Garrard County from S1c. Glen W. Cox (below) of Lancaster, who served on the USS *Panamint* AGC-13 with the Pacific Fleet in Sasebo, Japan, December 1945. (Courtesy Peggy Sharp.)

Serving on the USS *Panamint* with S1c. Glen Cox (left) was fellow Garrard Countian Roy Sherman Campbell, a machinist's mate. The ship left the Aleutian Islands August 14, 1945, for Japan. In Japanese waters, former enemy pilots directed them through the mine fields in the harbor. Not knowing of their mission, shipmates became suspicious when the Japanese came aboard, then watched as the formal occupation of Japan ceremony was held on their deck September 8. (Courtesy Peggy Sharp.)

Also in the Pacific, a homesick T5g. Robin "Red" Ray of Lancaster holds a photograph of his wife, Avis. Ray was with the 353rd Engineer Construction Battalion. (Courtesy Brenda Eason; additional information Doan Adkison.)

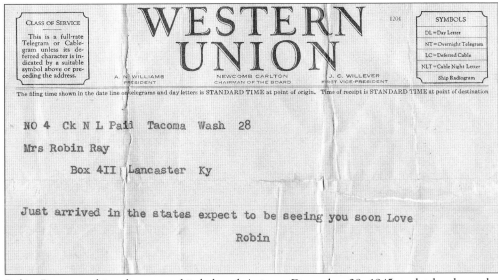

Robin Ray sent this telegram to his beloved Avis on December 28, 1945, to let her know he was coming home. He was discharged at Camp Atterbury, Indiana, on January 12, 1946. Camp Atterbury was where many Garrard County men were discharged. (Courtesy Norma Vanoy.)

A busy place during the occupation of Japan was the port of Yokohama and the army bases ashore. The above photograph shows the American barracks in the foreground and the city's port on Tokyo Bay beyond. (Courtesy Janice Blythe.)

Christian troops on and near the base worshiped in this chapel in Yokohama, which served both Catholics and Protestants, according to the sign. (Courtesy Janice Blythe.)

The Army Ground Forces (AGF) Band served as the musical ambassador of the troops. In the foreground, James H. "The Kid" (also known as "Brud" back home on Boones Creek) Burdette and members of the 16th AGF Band perform at a 71st Quartermasters Base football game in Yokohama, Japan. The others are not identified, but the band members included Arthur Barnett, Chicago (piano); Lester Bell, Toledo, Ohio (trombone); George Buckner, Detroit (drummer); Paul E. Cook, Beckley, West Virginia (drummer); Roosevelt Cray, Darby, Pennsylvania (trumpet); John Crenshaw, Chicago (tenor sax); Earl Faison, Detroit (no instrument listed); David R. Harrety, Roanoke, Virginia (drummer); John McClendon, Wheeling, West Virginia (alto sax); John R. Shannon, St. Paul, Minnesota (trumpet); Victor Sproles, Chicago (bass); and Jack Sutton, Chicago (saxophone). (Courtesy Janice Blythe.)

This Armistice Day parade was held in Yokohama on November 11, 1946. "A great day in Japan," wrote James H. Burdette in his scrapbook, "as the 16th Army Ground Forces Band marches by the reviewing stand." Burdette is indicated by the "me" in the photograph. His scrapbook included photographs of military trucks, other bands, and troops also marching down the street. (Courtesy Janice Blythe.)

James H. Burdette (second from left) and members of the 16th AGF Band donned parachutes and went up in planes as part of their training. "My father was a ground person and did not like having wings of angels," said Janice Burdette Blythe. From the air, he looked down on Mount Fuji, Japan's 12,500-foot mountain. (Courtesy Janice Blythe.)

While at the airport, James H. Burdette posed on one of the Japanese fighter planes confiscated by the United States after the war. (Courtesy Janice Blythe.)

Troops crowded the decks of the USAT *General J. H. MacRae* preparing to ship home to the States in May 1947 from the port of Yokohama in Tokyo Bay. (Courtesy Janice Blythe.)

This is the view James H. Burdette of Boones Creek saw as he lined up to board the USAT *General J. H. MacRae*. After nearly a year in Japan, part of which he spent in the hospital because of an operation, he was anxious to go home to family and friends. (Courtesy Janice Blythe.)

Seven

SOME GAVE ALL

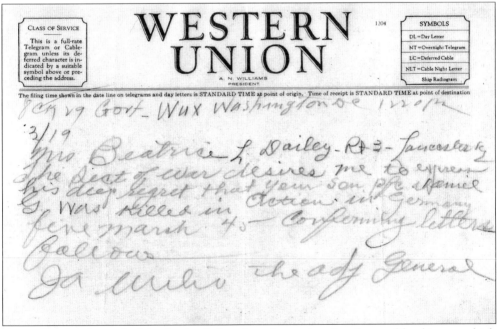

Next of kin first learned of the death of a loved one by receipt of a telegram like this one, which was sent to Beatrice Casey Dailey of Buckeye, informing her of the death of her oldest son, Daniel Glenmore Dailey, two weeks earlier in Germany. (Courtesy George Dailey.)

First Lt. Virgil Kinnaird Beasley was killed in action in Africa November 8, 1942. Before the invasion of French North Africa by American forces, he had been in command of an infantry company in Northern Ireland since June. Beasley graduated from Paint Lick High School and later from the University of Kentucky Law School (1941) as one of the leading students on the college's campus. (Courtesy Ruth McElveen.)

S.Sgt. Hobart Henry Spires of Bryantsville was killed in a B-17 Flying Fortress bomber over Berlin on March 6, 1944. Spires was in the top turret gunner position. A member of the Army Air Force, he joined the service in 1942 and flew with the 100th Bomb Group, 349th Squadron, based in England. (Courtesy Pete Arnold.)

Hobart Henry Spires posed on March 19, 1943, the day he married Frances Arnold in Bryantsville. He spent two weeks on leave with his bride then returned to Europe to continue his mission. Frances never saw him again. After the war, his body was returned in a closed casket to Bryantsville and he is now buried at Camp Nelson National Cemetery near the Jessamine-Garrard County border. (Courtesy Pete Arnold.)

Sgt. Clyde Stormes Layton was killed by a German mine on March 17, 1944 in Italy. Fellow soldier and buddy Lt. Harry D. Congers wrote Layton's parents, Jess and Osie Calico Layton, a week later saying he "was a real soldier and had many buddies who would miss him, and they would continue to fight for freedom." Layton had been in the army about two years; four months of those were spent overseas. The family would learn later that Congers was also killed in action. (Courtesy David and Frances Layton.)

Clyde Layton's parents received their last letter from their son on March 26, not knowing yet that he had been killed. He wrote that he was well and was in Italy. He was survived by six brothers and two sisters. His brother Bill was also in the service (see page 32). (Courtesy David and Frances Layton.)

Most if not all of these men were reported missing April 27, 1944, while on a reconnaissance mission from Wheeler Army Air Force Base in Hawaii. Radio contact with the plane was lost, and none of the crewmembers ever were found. Shown here are, from left to right, (first row) Clarence Blattner, waist gunner (Minnesota); Harmon Hess, waist gunner (Ohio); ? Duprey, tail gunner; Gordon B. Wilson, ball-turret gunner (Buena Vista, Kentucky); Lloyd Follis, engineer (Tennessee); and Francis Fraser, radio operator (Connecticut); (second row) ? McInerney, pilot; ? Stafford, navigator; George Simkulet, bombardier (New York); and Sidney Leeds, copilot (New York). All except Duprey, McInerney, and Stafford are listed among the missing on a World War II memorial wall of honor at the Honolulu Cemetery. Wilson was the oldest of three brothers who fought during the war. Brothers Hudson and Denver returned home safely. (Courtesy Paul Wilson family.)

S2c. Charles Garner Land was killed in the English Channel on April 28, 1944, during pre-D-Day maneuvers. The May 20, 1944, *Central Record* article announcing his death did not give a location or the date of death, probably because those details had not been released due to national security reasons. (Courtesy Edwin Land.)

S2c. Charles Garner Land of Buckeye was liked by all, said his brother, Edwin, especially older people. He loved horses and always had a horse or pony. He had volunteered for service in World War II, just as his father, Charlie Land, had done in World War I. Charles was only 18 years old at the time of his death. (Courtesy Edwin Land.)

Clarence Rhodus Jr. of Lancaster was sitting guard following the Battle of Normandy when a group of German soldiers pushed back through the American lines and killed him on July 18, 1944. Canadian soldiers found his body, and he was holding a photograph of his girlfriend and his New Testament. The soldiers sent the photograph to Rhodus's mother, Anna Elizabeth Smith Rhodus, but asked to keep the bible because there were many scriptures marked. "Maybe his death was not in vain," wrote his sister, Nora Bethel, "as those soldiers may have met the Lord through the scriptures." (Courtesy Nora Bethel.)

Pfc. George Washington Combs Jr. was killed in action at St. Lô, France on August 10, 1944. While drafted from Perry County, Kentucky, he lived in Garrard County on Old Wallaceton Road at one time. His younger brother, Donald, remembers George teaching him to read using the comics in the (Louisville) *Courier-Journal*. (Courtesy Jackie Lake.)

The Combs family lived in Wallaceton (Madison County) when George was home on his last leave. "Mom said he walked down the road, turned, and came back to hug me," wrote sister, Jackie, who was two years old then. "Mom knew that would be the last time she would ever see him." George Combs Jr. was first laid to rest in France. An American Red Cross volunteer sent this photograph of his grave. He is now buried at Berea Cemetery. (Courtesy Jackie Lake.)

Navy Fireman First Class Charles Gilbert Conn was killed in action October 14, 1944, in the boiler room on the USS *Houston* (CL-81). He "was manning his battle station in the aft fire room during an engagement with an organized enemy," wrote his commander. His body was not recovered until November 18, 1944. He had died of third-degree burns over his entire body by superheated steam and of asphyxiation by the steam. He was identified by his name on his clothing and a birthmark on his back. (Courtesy Nancy Cox.)

The parents of Charles Gilbert Conn received a letter with a statement of inventory for his personal effects, which included clothing, 38¢, photographs, souvenirs, an empty wallet, a box of stationery and stamps, a checkerboard set, and his New Testament. (Courtesy Nellie Hightower.)

Pvt. Woods Walker Lear of Cartersville was inducted into the army in late 1943 and served in the Asiatic Pacific theater. He was killed November 4, 1944, at Leyte Island, during the liberation of the Philippines. He was 25 years old and left behind a two-and-a-half-year-old son, Fred. His wife, Berniece Conn Lear, was pregnant with his daughter, Phyllis, who was born four months after his death. (Courtesy Fred Lear.)

Boyd Matlock was killed in action on December 9 or 10, 1944, in Northern Italy. A letter to his mother, Celie Creech Matlock, from the chaplain at his division headquarters reads, in part, "He was in a defensive position when enemy shells came into the company area, and he was struck and killed by shell fragments. . . . Your son was buried in a U.S. Military Cemetery in Northern Italy, and I conducted a simple Protestant battlefield service at his graveside. . . . (I)n giving his life for his country he made the 'supreme sacrifice.' " (Courtesy Phyllis Hicks)

T.Cpl. Delmas Lee McDonald of Bryantsville was killed in action on February 5, 1945, near a river north of Manila during a raid on a POW camp for Bataan Death March prisoners in the Philippines. He died while attacking a Japanese pillbox. "Somebody wrote his dad and said he didn't suffer," said cousin Barry Peel. "His buddies could not get to him. They had orders to change position right after he was shot. The next wave of infantry supposedly got all of the bodies and took them back to this prison camp, which had now been liberated. They buried them there where the Bataan people had been held." The photograph at right was taken early in his service, and the one below in the Pacific. He had been working in Ohio before the war. (Courtesy Barry Peel.)

Marine Claude Edward Montgomery was killed in action at Iwo Jima on February 20, 1945. This was the first invasion of Japanese soil and was one of the bloodiest battles in history. He is photographed here with unidentified neighbors during his last leave in Garrard County before shipping out overseas. (Courtesy Tommy Montgomery and Shirley Turner.)

Claude Edward Montgomery of Mount Hebron wanted to be a Marine from the time he was a boy, said his brother, Thomas "Tommy" Montgomery. "I was the last family member to see him alive," he said. "I took him to the train depot in Richmond. He wouldn't let me go inside and wait with him. And he wouldn't look back." (Courtesy Tommy Montgomery and Shirley Turner.)

Pfc. William Chester "Chigger" Bryant was killed in action in Belgium March 4, 1945. The son of Rev. and Mrs. W. H. Bryant of White Lick Baptist Church, he had entered the army on August 11, 1944, and was sent overseas in early January. Among survivors were his three-year-old son, Gary, and his wife, Marjorie Rhodus Bryant of Dayton, Ohio, whose brother, Clarence Rhodus Jr., was killed in action in July 1944. His body was returned to Garrard County and he was buried at Robinson Cemetery near Cartersville on May 31, 1949. (Courtesy Mary Ann Bolton.)

SCHOOL DAYS
1942-43

Daniel Glenmore Dailey, son of Dewey and Beatrice Casey Dailey, was a student at Buckeye High School in 1942–1943. His younger brother, George, said: "In 1941, daddy's right leg locked up and his kneecap burst. He went to Louisville in the latter part of the year to be operated on. Glenmore dropped out of school to tend the crop while dad was laid up." His father walked again, and Glenmore returned to school in the same class as younger brother Lloyd. They graduated together. (Courtesy George Dailey.)

Glenmore Dailey was dating Edwina Carter before his induction. Here they are at the entrance to Buckeye High School. "Soon after graduation, he was called upon to serve his country, and he did so proudly," wrote his nephew, Mark Dailey, in a letter to the *Central Record* editor decades after Dailey's death. (Courtesy George Dailey.)

Pfc. Glenmore Dailey was killed by a gunshot to the chest on March 5, 1945, near Euskirchen, Germany. His company had just taken Euskirchen and was preparing to attack the next town. While crossing an open field about 600 yards wide, they came under attack, and he was hit. He died before reaching the battalion aid station. (Courtesy Lloyd Dailey.)

Pfc. Daniel Glenmore Dailey initially was interred at Henri Chapelle Military Cemetery in Belgium about seven miles southwest of Aachen, Germany. The Allies refused to bury their dead on German soil. Photographs of the burial process at Henri Chapelle appeared in the May 1945 issue of *Life* magazine. Those graphic photographs of bodies lined up in preparation for burial must have been heartbreaking for the family to see. (Courtesy George Dailey.)

Above, the flag-draped casket of Pfc. Daniel Glenmore Dailey is carried by World War II veterans from his Poor Ridge Road home. Pallbearers, from left to right and front to back, are Clyde Long, Russell Ray, Leroy Davis (hidden), Eugene Grubbs, W. T. Casey, and Bobby Carter; the undertaker behind the casket and those on the lawn are unidentified. Below, Dailey's casket is carried into Liberty Baptist Church in Buckeye. Behind the casket are Glenmore's parents and siblings (from left to right) George, Carolyn, Ernest, and Lloyd Dailey. He was buried with full military honors in Lancaster Cemetery. (Courtesy George Dailey.)

Chester Dyehouse was killed by a sniper on June 4, 1945, in the Pacific. His sister-in-law, Inez Dyehouse, wrote: "Chester served in one of the thickest fighting zones in the Pacific. He had just received papers for a permanent discharge after three years overseas, when he was shot by a sniper on one of the islands in the Philippines." (Courtesy Inez Dyehouse.)

MEN FROM GARRARD COUNTY WHO DIED IN SERVICE DURING WORLD WAR II AND THE OCCUPATION PERIOD

Virgil Kinnaird Beasley
Ernest Blevins
Edwin P. Browning
William Chester Bryant
Henry C. Burnside
Ralph Gilbert Carpenter
Monroe Casey
George Washington Combs
Charles Gilbert Conn
Willard C. Currie
Daniel Glenmore Dailey
James S. Dailey
Chester Dyehouse
John D. Fathergill
David Faulkner
Bascom Evans Ford
Roy Bonaparte Halcomb
John R. Harris
Moses Helms
Luther Price Hughes
Herbert O'Neal Kelley
Walter Garnett Killion
Elias B. Kuykendall
Leroy Kuykendall

Charles Garner Land
Clyde Stormes Layton
Woods Walker Lear
Boyd W. Matlock
Julian Francis Matlock
Delmas Lee McDonald
Arthur Dewey Montgomery
Claude Edward Montgomery
William Moore
Walter Calvin Morris
William Cecil Parsons
Burnam Clayton Prather
Clarence Rhodus Jr.
Zachariah T. Rice III
Harry G. Sims
Hobart Henry Spires
James William Starnes
Eugene C. Sutton
Ed Harlan Swope
Stanley Tapp
Clyde Watkins
William Elisha West
Gordon Broaddus Wilson
Jack Wilson

A future book is planned to honor all who served in World War II from this county, both the fallen heroes and the ones who returned. Margaret Burkett and Rita Fox welcome names, photographs, and stories for anyone who lived in Garrard County before or during the war. If you can help with what will be a monumental resource and much-deserved tribute, please contact either of them.